MW00532302

If I Knew Then, What I Know Now!

College and Financial Aid Planning From A Parent's Perspective

If I Knew Then, What I Know Now!

College and Financial Aid Planning From A Parent's Perspective

Cynthia Hammond-Davis

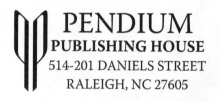

PENDIUM
PUBLISHING HOUSE
514-201 DANIELS STREET
RALEIGH, NC 27605

For information, please visit our Web site at
www.pendiumpublishing.com

PENDIUM Publishing and its logo
are registered trademarks.

If I Knew Then, What I Know Now!
College and Financial Aid Planning From A Parent's Perspective
By Cynthia Hammond-Davis

ISBN: 978-1-936513-33-8

PUBLISHER'S NOTE

This book is printed on acid-free paper.

Table of Contents

Acknowledgments

To my beautiful mother Olivia Wallace, I love you very much! Thank you dad, Bobby Wallace for all of your wisdom. To my awesome husband Ronald, my children Dana and Ronald, Jr., grandchildren, friends and family, thank you all very much for your love and support.

This book is dedicated
in loving memory of
Donna M. Williams-Davis

Foreword

This book is a treasure. It is the type of book that consistently has you walking away with a new gem of knowledge, a sense of discovery, and a renewed sense of purpose and mission. Cynthia Hammond Davis has taken the time to answer many of the questions that parents and students always wanted to ask and that those who have already moved through the higher education process wished they knew. *If I Knew Then, What I Know Now: College & Financial Aid Planning from a Parent's Perspective* is the type of book that finally provides a voice for many who typically would not even know to ask the question, but who would benefit immensely from the knowledge gained.

The higher education process is one that can be exceptionally difficult to navigate, especially if it is the first time that family may be encountering the process. Davis takes the time to address everything from the search and selection process to securing financial aid and merit scholarships with ease, and offers simple advice that will save parents and students alike precious time during the college admission process. She approaches the writing of this great piece in a way to offer advice in a reflective way that is not necessarily apologetic, but sincerely insightful as to how one can benefit from past experiences.

Within this book, the reader is invited to take a journey towards discovery that incorporates learning not only some of the benefits of planning early and asking the right questions, but also the importance of having open dialogue and communication among the family unit and the advantages of developing a support system while navigating the process. The support of family, teachers, and counselors has long been highlighted in higher education research as a positive factor in the successful pursuit of higher education, and Davis consistently reiterates that as a non-negotiable necessity for success. You are also invited to journey with Davis on her own path of reflection as she recounts the highs and lows of her experiences while navigating the college admission process.

It is exceptionally rare that you find an individual who is willing to be so candid to the point of sharing their personal experience and offering advice for the benefit of others at the cost of lessons learned. That is what is so authentic about the voice of this book; it comes from a place of passion for the work and genuine care and concern about the future generations of students and leaders of our world. Davis not only speaks about the issue in this book, but she stands in the gap for many of our children who will be the college students of tomorrow.

It is my hope that every parent and even students walk away from this book with the knowledge that there are many people who truly care about your success. These individuals have dedicated their lives to ensuring that you reach your educational and professional goals. Cynthia Hammond Davis is a giant among those fighting for your success. As a mentor, minister, and educator, she stands tall. As a concerned parent and dedicated advocate, she stands ready to help.

Enjoy the journey, and know that it is your responsibility to not only use what you will now know, but to share it with someone else so they will not be left behind.

James B. Massey Jr.
Senior Associate Director
Office of Undergraduate Admissions
University of Maryland, College Park

Introduction

A white package with maroon-colored print and a picture of a hawk sat on the dining room table from the college my son had applied. I could hardly wait for my son to get home from school. I wanted to rip it open, but I waited. We (my husband, son, and daughter) opened it together and were excited to see the word "Congratulations!" Our son had been accepted to college! We immediately called family and friends who shared our excitement.

I thoroughly read the letter to make sure I knew the next steps that needed to be taken. It explained the importance of sending a three-hundred-dollar deposit to reserve a bed in one of the campus dorms. It also talked about the importance of filling out a form called the FAFSA (Free Application for Federal Student Aid) if we needed assistance with financing, and we definitely did.

We picked up a FAFSA form from my son's high school and began filling it out. It was a very difficult form with over one hundred questions. In 2000, the federal government did not have the online version of the form yet. So, we had to fill the form out and mail it in. I did the best I could with it, carefully checking the figures I inserted in the little boxes. When I got to the part that read, "How much money do you have in your savings and checking account today?" I chuckled and put a small amount in the box.

My husband and I worked for a public school system. In 2000, I worked as a school secretary in the counseling department at a middle school, and my husband worked as a supply worker. We were support service employees. When my son's Student Aid Report (SAR)* came in the mail about four weeks later, our Expected Family Contribution (EFC)** was listed as 10004. We had no idea what this EFC was or what it would do. So, we accepted it for what it was and did nothing to change it. We could have put in the wrong information, but still we did nothing because we didn't know anything about EFC's or what it meant.

I found out later that the number listed as the EFC is an estimate of how much the government says you can afford to contribute to your child's tuition per year. Our EFC of 10004 meant that $10,004 per year is what we were expected to contribute! My first thought was, *Oh my goodness! What?! How in the world can we afford to pay ten thousand dollars per year for our son's tuition?* Based on their calculations, this meant we needed little help paying for our son's college tuition, because in 2000, this particular college's cost of attendance was approximately $15,000 per year. That's probably the reason why we received our financial aid package full of loan applications!

A couple weeks later, we received another letter from the school. This envelope had approximately five or six sheets of paper in it. The first page was the award letter, which informed us of how much money they could provide based on our EFC. In the middle of the page were two columns that showed the breakdown of the costs. The left column listed the Cost of Attendance (COA), including tuition, room & board, fees, room deposit, etc. On the right side of the paper were words I had never seen before, such as subsidized loans and unsubsidized loans. It also listed the balance that the loans and grants didn't cover, which was somewhere around $5,000.00. Included in the award letter was the option for my husband and me to apply for a Parent PLUS Loan if we couldn't pay the balance out of pocket. Since we didn't have the money, we filled out the papers and accepted all of the loans. My son signed, we signed, and then mailed it back in. We were approved for the loan, and my son was on his way to college.

However, when we looked at the financial aid award letters my son received, I knew we were in trouble. Why? Because I was still unsure of what it said! I didn't know how to read it! I was excited and disappointed at the same time. My son received the majority of his financial aid in loans, he had bowling scholarship money from tournaments that totaled several thousand dollars but we had to fill out a Parent PLUS Loan to meet the rest of the tuition costs. The good news, my son was going to college! *Yay!* The bad news, we were not financially prepared and had a lot of money to pay!

What about our financial needs? Since we didn't make a lot of money, why didn't we receive more scholarships and/or grants? What about all of the billions of dollars in scholarships that are out there? How in the world will we be able to afford the yearly EFC that the federal government calculated? How long will it take to pay off these loans?

These were some of the questions I really wanted someone to answer, but who could I speak with? I didn't have the slightest idea. When we spoke with the college financial aid officer who asked a lot of questions about our FAFSA, tax information, etc., their response began and ended with the "L" word, LOANS! We signed papers and promissory notes that we really didn't understand. "Is there anyone here who can help us understand all of this stuff?" I asked, but all I heard was silence. No one could help us understand why we had to pay so much money. Again, we were not prepared. We had not counted up all of the costs of tuition ahead of time. We waited too late.

I know how most of you must be feeling as you are reading this. You may be asking how you and/or your spouse will be able to afford to send your child(ren) to college. That's the reason why I decided to write this book. I hope you find some of your answers in these pages. If you find at least one thing that helps, I've done my job and am pleased. Parents, please take the time to research, and please start earlier than we did. Senior year was entirely too late for us to start.

*SAR = Student Aid Report is a form you will receive from federal student aid after your FAFSA has been processed. It shows all of the information you entered on your FAFSA form. Check it out thoroughly for any mistakes you may have made. If you find mistakes, go to the FAFSA. gov website and correct your saved/processed FAFSA. The good news is you will receive the SAR much faster now that everything is processed online. The SAR will be emailed to you shortly after you have completed the online FAFSA.

**EFC =Expected Family Contribution is a figure the federal government calculates from your income, assets, etc. for the parents and also the student if the student worked, as well. It is an estimate, according to the federal government calculations, of what the family should be able to contribute to their child's tuition.

Dear Parents,

I am writing this book because just like you, I have experienced overwhelming anxiety, stress, and sleepless nights with concerns of college planning, thinking about where my children would attend college, and wondering how we would be able to pay for it. I write this book with you in mind and hope you will not make some of the same mistakes I did. I hope you will start learning about the college and financial aid process early in your child's life. If your child decides to attend a career-focused or technical school, you still need to know about the financial aid process, because although funding may be available through the federal government and other organizations, it may not be enough for them to be completely debt free.

I titled the book *If I Knew Then What I Know Now, College & Financial Aid Planning from a Parent's Perspective* because as a parent, I have been where you are now. I had so many questions, but could not find answers. *What's the best college for my children? Where are the scholarships? How much financial aid will I receive? For what do I qualify? For what do my children qualify? Where can I go to find assistance?* The counselors at my children's school were very good at helping us find colleges and a few organizational scholarship applications, but where could we find help with financial aid planning? Which of the 3,600 or more colleges would fit my child?

We couldn't find answers to our questions. I went to the college financial aid office thinking they would help us find scholarships and grants, but we received only a little grant money and scholarships. We were offered more loans than anything. By the way, grants and scholarships DO NOT have to be paid back.

I wrote this book to share with you where I found help and continue to seek help. There are great places on the internet and resource books that can help you with this process. The only problem I find is that some of these places on the internet and resource books use language that may be very confusing to the average parent and student who are not familiar with the financial aid and college terminology. Terms like Cost of Attendance (COA) or Expected Family Contribution (EFC) can be very confusing to a parent and student. I am going to make every attempt to break the language down so you can understand it.

I also wrote this book because this is my passion and I absolutely love young people! Every time I see a child or teenager in a store, mall, or restaurant, I have an urge to ask them, "So, where do you plan to attend college?" And sometimes I do. My husband and I have done this on several occasions. He is a NCAA Division 1 coach and always looking for prospective student athletes. I won't mention what sport he coaches or where because that's not the purpose of the book. The purpose of the book is to help you become familiar with the college and financial aid process. I hope I have said something in this book that will lead you to a better understanding of the process and that you come out knowing a bit more than you did before reading it. If I've done that, I have met my goal in helping you become more knowledgeable of this whole college and financial aid maze.

Feel free to let me know if the book helped you. If you have a question or would like to make a comment about the book, my email address is ***hammonddavisllc@yahoo.com.***

Sincerely,
Cynthia Hammond Davis

Dear Prospective College or Technical School Student,

Thank you for taking the time out of your busy schedule to read this book. I hope it will help you during your search for the college that best fits you, along with the financial aid planning that comes with the decision to attend college.

I cannot stress enough how important it is to keep your grades up. Do the very best you can! If you attend a public school, take advantage of this free education we have in the United States, and for those who are in a private school, please be grateful for the ones paying your tuition and do the very best you can in your academics. When speaking with college representatives, I always ask them what type of students "best fit" their school, and most of them will say a student who has done the best they can in their academics, in their community, and in extracurricular activities. So, I encourage you to take courses that challenge you to think more, to study more and get involved in your community.

Please communicate with your counselor and teachers. They are your best advisors along with your parents. Teachers know your academic strengths and weaknesses. They are there to help you learn and master your subjects. Do not be afraid to ask for help. Most teachers love when students ask for their help; they see you have a willingness to learn. If you are shy or maybe too embarrassed to ask your teacher a question in front of everyone, utilize your email! Most schools have websites with all of the staff's email addresses. Email your teachers. Give them a day or two to answer because they may have a lot of students on their roster who are doing the same. So, be patient. Also, please get in touch with your counselors. Make an appointment with them. If possible, have your parents attend the meeting with you. Let your counselor know that you plan to attend college. Do this as early as 9th grade in high school or even in middle school!

I hope this book serves as a guide in your quest to attend college and how to pay for it. I hope you reach all of your academic goals and become a great asset to your community.

If you have a question or would like to make a comment about the book, please email me at *hammonddavisllc@yahoo.com.* Thank you again for your time in reading this.

Sincerely,
Cynthia Hammond Davis

Chapter One

Teamwork Is The Key!

While they were growing up, our kids were our life. I don't think I would have changed anything about how involved we were with them, just more involved in their academic achievements and making sure both of them knew the importance of a college education or a career-focused school.

Remember, as a family, you are a team! Teamwork is the key to a successful college planning experience. Having a heart-to-heart conversation with your children before researching colleges is imperative.

If I knew then what I know now, we would have had a heart-to-heart conversation with our children. We would have sat them down before they started looking at colleges and told them exactly how much we could contribute. We would have shared our monthly income and expenses with them so they could see exactly how much we had left after paying our monthly bills. Doing this early may have also opened our eyes to see where we could have saved more. (I'll explain this in a later chapter.) We would have explained to our children that they had a part to play in this process, as well. Their part was to do the very best in their academics, and study hard. They did that. However, if I knew then the importance of the SAT/ACT test scores, I would have paid for a tutor or a test prep company to help them prepare, so they would be a good candidate for academic/merit-based college scholarships. Doing this may have saved us thousands of dollars!

I had no idea what colleges cost or what I would have to contribute. We were under the impression that if we didn't have the money to pay, we would receive financial aid grants or scholarships. Boy was I mistaken! Having a heart-to-heart talk with my children upfront before they started looking at colleges may have saved us thousands of dollars! I repeat this with emphasis! I blame myself partly because I left this very important part of our lives up to someone else instead of doing the research myself. We just assumed the counselors at the high school would help us figure this all out and that the government and/or college would help us pay most of it, leaving us with only a small portion to pay. But, that was wrong of us to do. That's why I try hard to get the message out to everyone that I possibly can so you, parents and students, will be prepared and not shocked at the REAL cost of college, and hopefully, you'll avoid ending up in so much debt like us.

One thing I can say, I was very involved in the PTSA (also known as PTO, PTA or other parent organization) at my children's school, because I believe as a family we are a team. However, if I knew then what I know now, I would have taken advantage of the great relationship I built with the school staff and sought help from them for my children's academic strengths and struggles. The PTSA gives you a chance to speak with the principal and other key personnel about the things happening in the school. It's a time to talk about what's right, what's wrong, and what needs to improve. It's a time to get questions answered. If I knew then what I know now, I would have taken more time off my job to visit my children at school, whether they liked it or not. This would have given me an opportunity to see firsthand how they worked in certain subjects and with certain teachers. They were our responsibility, and we owed it to them to be involved in every area of their lives.

I remember visiting my daughter and son's classes during the annual Open House, a day when parents can attend school with their child. Some schools have an Open Door Policy that allows parents to observe classroom instruction at any time. Check into this! I was one of very few parents who came to the Open House event.

At one particular middle school, my son and a group of other students went to the same classes together every day. It was amazing to watch the same students go from class to class, but act differently in each one. In the first class—let's say it was math, but I honestly can't remember—the teacher gave them an assignment, and the students worked on it. Some students would talk with each other, get out of their seat to go to the pencil sharpener, or become a distraction for others in some way. When the teacher would ask them to return to their seats, they would very slowly make it back to their assigned seat and continue working on their assignment. The bell rang, and we went to another class, where the teacher lectured to them. Some of the students had their heads down on their desks, some were talking loudly and ignoring the teacher, while others were on task. My son, knowing I was there, stayed on task, but I often wondered what really happened when I wasn't there. *Hmmm.* In that particular class, the kids were loud and sometimes out of control. The teacher didn't seem to have any classroom management skills, and the students knew it. So, they acted accordingly.

The bell rang, and we went to the English class. This class I remember vividly like it was yesterday. After the students sat in their assigned seats, the middle-aged male teacher began sharing a story with them that was intriguing. All of the students were very attentive. I can't remember what he said, but I was very interested, too. He talked about a book they were about to read, and he made it sound so interesting that I was ready to read it! After he introduced the book, he said, "Now let's open up our book to see and read what happens next." I started looking for a book so I could read along!

There was no noise, no students out of their seats, no talking at all; just reading. These were the same students who were totally out of control in the last class, but now they were sitting and reading attentively! What happened? Well, it was definitely the English teacher's approach to the students and the way he caught their attention. He also seemed to have his classroom under control. I admired that.

The next day, the principal invited parents to a meeting with teachers, staff, and administration about the climate of the school. When I was asked if I had something to say, I mentioned the classrooms I visited and teachers I observed on Open House day. Being careful not to point fingers, I expressed how I thought there was a classroom management issue in some of the classes I visited. How would I know if I didn't visit the classroom? So, I urge parents who are reading this book to sit in a class at least once or twice a year if at all possible. This is teamwork at its best. My children still remember times when I showed up at their school. Most of the time it was for good reasons, because they knew they could count on us to be there. We visited my son and daughter's classes, yes, even in high school! Look, I totally understand some parents reading this book cannot take off work as easily as others, but if you can't take a day off work, find someone who you trust very well to take your place at Open House days. It may be a relative, friend, church member, but it is imperative that you know what's going on in the classroom. Some public schools may have class sizes of twenty to forty students to one teacher. You need to make sure your child is receiving the best education possible.

If I knew then what I know now, I would have made sure I checked my children's schoolwork every night. It is imperative that you stay on top of this. Teachers can only do so much. We, as parents, have to do our part, as well. If you do not understand the material your child is bringing home, seek assistance from the teacher, a college student, an older sibling, or an older high school person who may be able to assist. Do not forget to do this. Homework may be a huge part of the grading process, so you want to make sure your child is doing everything he or she can to complete all assignments, including homework.

If I knew then what I know now, I would have made sure there was a balance in extracurricular activities, homework, church, and other events that took place outside the home. I remember attending organizational meetings, basketball and football games, but I never checked to see if my children's homework had been completed. Parents, make sure you don't make this mistake. Check your child's homework; make sure it's done. Look at their plan books or homework assignment pages. Some schools have weekly student progress reports available on their websites. Make sure you are checking them. If you do not have a computer at home, have a friend print it out and bring it to you.

You must make every effort to stay on top of everything! As I've stated before, if you do not know how to check the school's website or do not have a computer, I encourage you to seek help from someone who does. There are many of us who attend social activities. Seek the assistance of college students or young adults who you trust. Some schools, and nonprofit organizations offer free tutoring. Take advantage of it! Please!

I scheduled reading time for an hour a day with no television or phones allowed. If my children did not have homework, their assignment from me was to find an interesting article in the newspaper at least three or four paragraphs in length, read it, and then write it. This helps so much with reading, spelling, grammar, punctuation, and more.

Parents, if I knew then what I know now, I would have looked for my child's strengths in academics and sharpened them by making sure they mastered the material. Then, most importantly, I would have looked for their weaknesses and had a teacher or tutor work with them to help strengthen those areas. We did this, but I believe we could have done more in this area. These are mistakes I do not want you to follow.

Chapter Two

Find Your Gifts/Talents, Abilities/ Strengths & Passion

When I talk with students I let them know they have gifts, talents, strengths, skills and passion. I help students tap into those gifts and other abilities by building a relationship with them. I use resource tools on the internet that have career interest surveys. The internet is great resource for this! Students can take a career interest survey answering questions about their likes and dislikes. After the student completes the survey, a list of careers based on interests will be listed for the student to research further.

I tried my best to look for my children's gifts and talents. I believe they are in the right jobs. My son is an IT Specialist. His major in college was computer science. When he's working on computers, he is in his element. It's like he was born to do this and he does it for family and friends, sometimes without charge. He's as passionate about his career as I am about assisting students and parents with college and financial aid planning. My daughter's gift is in social and health services and I believe that's the right career for her.

Here's what I say to parents and students:

Think back a bit when you were younger.

- What did you love to pay with or do?
- Do you find yourself doing these same things today?
- Would you do this even if there were no money to pay you for it?

This may be a gift, passion or skill. If you can build a major and career around your gifts, talents, strengths, skills and passion you may love what you do as a career for a long time. Let me give you an example:

As a child, as early as I can remember, I always talked to an imaginary audience. I would talk about anything. I would pretend to be the guest speaker talking with thousands and thousands of people. Sometimes I would sing. I can remember doing this as early as age five! I can vividly see myself standing near a wooded area, talking and singing, with the trees as my audience. Funny, isn't it?

Well today, I am a motivational speaker and have been talking in front of audiences on a weekly basis for over 20 years. Little did I know, as early as age five I was practicing and perfecting my gift of public speaking! I am also a former radio talk show host, speaking to thousands of people on the air. "The College & Career Information Hour" aired every Saturday morning from 8:00-9:00a.m. (EST) on WOL, a Radio One station. If you live in the Washington DC area, you may have been able to tune into 1450AM on your radio. In addition, I host college and financial aid workshops, speaking with parents and students. Wow! Isn't that amazing?

And, guess what? I still speak to my imaginary audience almost every day! It is my hope to travel around the nation speaking about this book to audiences small and large. That's only one of my many gifts/skills, talents and abilities. So, to answer my own questions:

- What did you love to play with or do as a child?
  A: Talk and sing to an imaginary audience.
- Do you find yourself doing those same things today?
  A: Yes

- Would you do this even if there were no money to pay you ?
  A: Yes, I sure have and still do at times!

Now, how about your children. Think back when your children were younger. What brought them the most joy? Think about those things that came naturally to them. It could have been building blocks, writing, reading, completing word puzzles, having an interest in the environment, gardening, singing, dancing, drawing, painting, taking things apart and putting them back together, cooking or trying to figure out how a computer game works just to name a few. I know that I am working in my gift because when I help parents and students with college and financial aid planning, I am in my "zone" I am energized, full of excitement and enthusiasm, and I experience such pleasure knowing that I am helping someone achieve their goals. When I am speaking in front of an audience I sometimes say to myself, this is what I've been preparing for all these years! I love standing before a crowd! I always love to poll my audience to see who is in the room and how I can best reach each and every one of them at their level, age or grade of their child. I honestly feel like I am playing and working at the same time! I am completely fulfilled. That's when you know you are working in your passion! I've had jobs that I hated. I was exhausted when I got there and exhausted when I left. I was not happy nor did I have a sense of fulfillment, but since I have totally allowed myself to follow my dreams, I know this is what I was born to do! Because of my love for reading and writing, it took no time to write this book because it has been in me for so long, waiting to get out!

If I knew then what I know now, I would have observed my children more closely to see what things came natural to them and helped them master that skill, gift, talent and ability. My daughter is a very loving individual who passionately concerns herself with the health, care and well being of others. If I knew then what I know now, I would have sought more help from her counselors, teachers, and others who knew her well. I would have asked them about internships and volunteer opportunities in social services or the health field. My daughter is a beautiful person who will prosper in anything she does because she honestly cares about people. Watch your children to see what they like to do on a daily basis. What do you find them doing most? What strengths do you see in them? What weaknesses?

Watch your children closely and look for their gifts, talents and abilities. Does your child play doctor with their dolls or stuffed animals? Speak to an imaginary audience? When my granddaughter was about four or five years old, she would place all of her dolls on the floor and pretend to be a teacher. Maybe one of her gifts, talents, abilities is teaching. My grandson talks a lot, all the time. He has an answer for everything and is very inquisitive. He loves watching television shows that have attorneys or people who advocate for others. I think he would make a great attorney or child advocate or something in that field.

I know students who from a very young age knew they wanted to go into the armed forces. Some of them went through ROTC programs at their high school and/or attended a college with an ROTC program and received scholarship money that helped pay their tuition. For more information about ROTC programs, check out the "Resources" page in the back of this book.

Students, there are websites I would like you to check out. Use a search engine to look for Naviance Family Connections or other career websites that may be available. One of the many features on this website is the Career Interest Survey. This survey may help you figure out what careers and majors interest you based on your gifts, talents, abilities, likes and dislikes.

After filling out the general registration information, you should be able to start the survey. It should take about twenty minutes or so to complete. Take your time and answer the questions to the best of your ability. After you have finished the quiz, check out some of the careers that match your interests by clicking on the name of the career. It will give you general information about the skills and education needed for the career, as well as provide you with current salary earnings. It also gives you a list of related careers.

Try it! The results may surprise you. Parents are you pursuing your dreams? What gifts, talents, abilities, likes and dislikes are inside of you? Take the quiz. You might be surprised of the results.

The most important thing to remember, not only is it necessary for your children to go college or some postsecondary school, but it is also necessary to be able to find a job when they graduate! Some students are leaving college with a huge amount of debt and no job in sight! This debt cannot be dismissed through bankruptcy and could cause a lot of financial problems if the loan is placed in default. That's why it's important to follow your passion. Build a career around that. For example if you love to investigate things and ask questions or love watching law programs on television and think you may want to be an attorney, try applying for an internship at a law office while you are in high school and or college. Don't worry too much about getting paid at this point. The experience is priceless!

Learn, observe and take good notes during your internship. Ask a lot of questions about the business. Look at all of the different positions in the law office. Internships could lead to temporary positions while you are in college and permanent positions after graduation. The great thing about internships, it allows you to see what you may be doing in your career. If your gifts, talents and skills are not being used, you will know sooner if this is really what you want to do as a career.

Do what you love! Follow your dreams! If you are really passionate about what you are doing, the money will follow. It may take some time. You may have to work more than one job for a while. I work long hours in my business because I absolutely love what I do! I'll say this again, it's like working and playing at the same time. I find myself so full of energy knowing that I've helped a student receive a huge scholarship or get into the college of their choice. I remember when my first client received $150,000 from the college of her choice. We were so excited. I don't think I slept that night because I was so excited about my accomplishment and felt a sense of purpose knowing that this was definitely my passion and I knew that I would do this for a very long time. I am winning and helping others to win! It took me many years to finally realize my purpose, my passion, but it doesn't have to take that long. If you follow your gifts, strengths, talents and passion you may love what you do and where you work for a long time.

Chapter Three

The Importance Of Good Grades & SAT/ACT Scores

If I knew then what I know now, I would have made sure to sign my children up for an SAT or ACT test prep class outside of school. The test prep classes in school are good, but I would have definitely forked up the money for the services of a local one-on-one test prep company. Check with your children's high school. They may have a listing of private tutors or local test prep companies that specialize in SAT/ ACT prep. If I knew then what I know now, this could have saved us thousands of dollars in loans. We had the money, but didn't realize it until it was too late. (Again, I'll explain this in detail in a later chapter.) There are many test prep companies from which to choose, but since I do not want to take up too much time from your busy schedule, I am only going to identify two. One of the companies I am familiar with is Revolution Prep, but do your research as well.

In 2002, Revolution Prep was founded with the vision of transforming education and remaining true to a social mission to make test prep accessible to all students. In 2009, over 48,000 students trusted Revolution Prep for academic tutoring and test prep. Revolution Prep wanted to provide the highest quality instruction to all students regardless of their ability to pay. Revolution Prep continues to give over two million dollars annually to students to help them prepare for the SAT and ACT.

By building a team of smart people dedicated to this vision, Revolution Prep created innovative methods and curricula that lead to student's success not just for tests but also in the future. From their social mission of never turning a student away because he or she could not afford the program, to company service days and partnership programs, Revolutionaries are committed to making a difference in their communities.

Revolution Prep uses online resources to personalize learning and train their instructors to infuse energy into every class to engage their students. Revolution Prep is passionate about what they do and students and parents experience this in every interaction they have with this group of people.

Please visit **www. revolutionprep.com** or call 1-877-738-7737 to view schedules for SAT/ACT classes that may be available in your area, says Nichole Leonard, Revolution Prep Regional Manager of DC/Maryland

Other options for students are websites like **www.collegeboard. org or ACT.org**. They may have free full-length practice tests and quizzes that students can complete to see which test fits them. There may be other test prep companies online that can help students prepare. Never take the SAT or ACT without practicing for it! Practicing this test may increase your scores on the actual test. I advise students to take the quiz on the website before taking the online practice test. Practice as much as you can and then take one of the free full-length practice tests. You do not have to take the test all at once. You can start and stop as you please. However, you should plan to spend some time doing each section, because it will show the child's weak areas and ways to strengthen them.

As I stated before, but it's worth mentioning again, a lot of colleges and universities use these tests to determine a student's college readiness, and sometimes the tests are used to determine who will receive academic (merit-based) scholarships. For example, *www.cappex.com* is a great website that lists scholarships available at the college or universities. Choose the state of your choice and then the college to see how much you may be eligible for. For example, The University of Maryland located in College Park, Maryland, has a scholarship called The Banneker Key. Locate it on *www.cappex.com*, (or another website if this is no longer available) to see how much a student may receive if he/ she fits the criteria.

If you want to know where the real money is, it's at the colleges and universities. Check the college website to make sure the scholarship is still being offered and to see if the criteria have changed. It's good to research this early when your children are in the 9th or 10th grade to see what types of GPAs and SAT/ACT scores are needed to obtain some of these scholarships so they can start practicing for the PSAT early! Some school districts will administer the PSAT (practice SAT) to students in the 10th grade and again in the 11th grade for National Merit Scholarship Qualification. This national merit scholarship program may lead students to additional scholarship money available through colleges and other organizations.

If I knew then what I know now, I would have insisted that my children take one or two honors and/or AP classes in their strongest subjects. Honors courses challenge the student to do more work than regular or on-level courses. For example, if a student is strong in English, an Honors English class will involve more reading and writing than a regular class. An AP class is a college-level class that students can take in high school. I cannot tell you how important reading and writing is in college. I talk with college students all the time who tell me that taking honors or AP classes helped prepare them for the rigorous classes in college, especially the massive amounts of reading and writing that may be required.

Again, if I knew then what I know now, I would have put my children in an SAT or ACT prep class. Back then, I knew nothing about the ACT, but I should have. I should have asked or listened when counselors talked about the national tests. These national tests are very important and used in a variety of ways by colleges. Some colleges look at them closely, while others do not, but you always want to be prepared either way.

I know students who have scored well (600, 700 and even a perfect score of 800 on each section) and have received significant academic/merit-based scholarship money from colleges. The highest score on each of the three sections of the SAT (Critical/ Verbal Reading, Math, and Writing) is 800 each, with a combined score of 2400. However, some schools are not adding the writing score yet. That's very important to know. Make sure to check with the colleges to see if they are including all three sections in their SAT requirement. If not, delete the writing score and add only the Critical Reading and Math scores. The ACT top composite score is 36. Students with high scores may receive academic or merit scholarships, but this varies from college to college. The SAT and ACT may change periodically, so make sure you know the changes and how the test is being scored.

All colleges are different. Some colleges do not look at SAT or ACT scores at all and may provide academic/merit based scholarships as well. Check out *www.fairtest.org* and view the list of colleges/universities that do not require these scores. Also, some colleges/universities allow students to 'opt out' of the test score requirement. Look at this website for accurate information, and please note that this information may change yearly.

Academic/merit-based scholarships are great and sometimes can be awarded for as much as full tuition, which may or may not include room, board, fees, books, etc. There is a lot to learn about academic scholarships. Most of them come with requirements that must be met by the student annually (every year). The student may have to maintain a certain GPA (Grade Point Average) each year. They may have to study a specific major, play a specific sport, etc. It is imperative that you read the fine print about the scholarship before signing.

Chapter Four

Extracurricular Activities, Community Service, and Summer Opportunities

"Extracurricular activities and community service are both instrumentalpiecesofasuccessfulcollegeapplication.Extracurricular activities provide additional insight as to who the student really is and what their passion involves. We are also able to understand how the student spends their time outside of the classroom and what type of activities may be important to them on a college campus that they may select. Community service is also important as it leads a student to understand the value of civic engagement. Our students of today are truly our leaders of tomorrow, and they must be prepared to understand the challenges within the communities in which they exist to truly affect positive and progressive change. Additionally, it is exceptionally important that students take advantage of summer academic or professional enrichment opportunities to maximize their time outside of the classroom. This may take the form of paid or unpaid internships (remember, the experience gained is the key!), study abroad trips, or even focused and intense volunteer work. It is in the best interest of the student to always use their free time wisely as

it is a welcomed opportunity to build their portfolio as they prepare for the college admission process. Many colleges and universities also offer summer academic enrichment programs for rising high school juniors and seniors that will introduce them to the learning environment in a university setting. Programs such as The Young Scholars Program at Maryland provide opportunities for students to benefit from structured academic experiences on a college campus— even before the college admission process."" says Mr. James Massey, Senior Associate Director, Undergraduate Admissions, University of Maryland, College Park.

Colleges and organizations look at community service as a great asset on a student's resume or application. Some organizations that provide scholarships to students may have the essay topic relate to community service. Colleges may look for community service on the students resume or use it as an essay topic, as well. Please be sure you are involving your children in community service.

I must say I ensured that my children participated in community service opportunities while attending high school. It was an awesome experience for students. They had to work at a soup kitchen preparing and serving meals to the homeless as part of their requirements for graduation. After their assignment was completed, the students wrote about their experiences at the soup kitchen. Both of my children began caring deeply about homeless men and women, and would continue this service periodically after they graduated. My daughter has continued this tradition with her children. Every year, they help prepare and serve meals to the homeless and elderly during the Thanksgiving and Christmas holidays.

If I knew then what I know now, I would have placed my children in more extracurricular activities. We did this, but just want to encourage others to do the same. My daughter was involved in drama/theatre, choir, cheerleading and bowling, while my son participated in JV and Varsity basketball, football and bowling.

Because of my son's love of bowling, he became a part of the coaching staff of the women's bowling team as a volunteer at his college. Why? The college did not have a men's bowling team, only an NCAA women's bowling team and a very good one! The year he joined the team as a volunteer junior assistant coach, they won the MEAC (Middle Eastern Atlantic Conference) tournament. He still has his college MEAC championship ring! The next year, he started a men's bowling club organization on campus and traveled to men's tournaments with other college club sports. They did not receive scholarship money, but they received funds from the school for tournament fees, travel, hotel, food, etc. The guys really didn't care. They just wanted to bowl, and that's what they did.

An amazing thing happened the year my son attended college as a freshman. The college opened their new student building. In that building, they added a new bowling alley, and guess who ran it? Yes, my son, and he got paid for it! Hallelujah! His gift and passion for bowling paid off in the end. His community service turned into a part-time job.

If I knew then what I know now, I would have had a mentor for both of my children. I had to face the fact that sometimes my children did not want to hear what I had to say. It's funny how parents can say something to them about college, and it goes in one ear and out the other. But, when someone else comes along and says the same exact thing you said, they listen. Has that happened to you? It's happened to us many times!

I would have found someone we all trusted to keep them motivated in high school and in college. Mentors serve a crucial role in keeping students motivated. A mentor could be a friend of the family, a relative, or another adult who you know and trust to encourage your child to fulfill their educational goals. Having your child participate in extracurricular activities, community service, and summer programs can also be a great place to find adult mentors who may be in the career field that your child is interested.

Chapter Five

Student Athletes–NCAA Collegiate Sports

If I knew then what I know now, I would have definitely had my daughter more involved in sports, especially bowling. My family bowled in leagues. My son was a great basketball and football player in high school, but a much better bowler. The only problem with that is scholarships are only available to women bowling teams at Division I and II colleges and universities. As I stated before, unfortunately, colleges do not have Division I and II bowling for men, which means no athletic scholarships were available to him. Why didn't I know that? Why didn't someone tell me?

If I knew then what I know now, I would have insisted that my daughter become more consistent in bowling. She was a good bowler. I had no idea that bowling scholarships were available for women. How did I miss that?

So, for all of you parents of athletes out there, become very familiar with the NCAA process, early! I had no idea about the NCAA process when my children were in school, but I know quite a bit now since I assist students with the registration process.

There are three divisions in the NCAA (National Collegiate Athletic Association); they are Division I, II, and III. The official website is *www.ncaa.org.* On the website, you can find information about how to register, which divisions give scholarships and which ones don't, signing the amateurism statement, and all of the requirements needed to qualify for the NCAA Clearinghouse. There is a guidebook that you can download on the website called *Guide for the College Bound Student Athlete.* This book gives you all the information you need to know about qualifications, GPA and ACT/SAT requirements, etc. You can download the book free of charge.

Parents and students, if I knew then what I know now, I would have planned ahead when thinking about collegiate sports. College coaches are looking for student athletes who can help their team win. I would have done my research. I would not have sent out tapes (CD's, DVD's) and randomly emailed coaches about my child's interest in their team without taking the time to look up the coach's name on the website. Please don't do what I did. Do your homework! Here are some things I would have done.

1) I would have researched colleges that fit my children both academically and athletically. I would have looked at the college website admissions page to see the admissions requirements, along with the minimum and average GPA & SAT scores. If my child was currently on the high school track team, for example, we would have compared our child's stats to the time and stats of current student athletes on the college's athletic website to see if they fit or not on the team? Were their stats at the top, middle, or bottom?

2) I would have counted the number of student athletes who were seniors on the college roster. The college seniors would not have been there when my child arrived as a freshman, which meant there might have been space on the team. Counting the juniors would have told us how many student athletes would be seniors and may have only had one year left to play. If most of the student athletes who played on the team were seniors and juniors, leaving only a few freshmen

and sophomores remaining, they may have had a need for more people on the team.

If I had researched correctly and had my children apply to the colleges where their academic and athletic ability were above or at least the same as the current student athletes, it may have helped them receive an athletic scholarship. There are student athletes whose academics and athletic talent may help them receive a partial or full athletic scholarship. Grades and talent are key! Remember, your children are students first and athletes second. That's the reason you will see the term "student athlete" throughout the NCAA Clearinghouse website. Also, athletic scholarships are awarded annually and may be renewed each year. There are requirements that students have to meet in order to maintain their eligibility for the scholarship.

If your child exceeds the stats of the current college student athletes AND has the GPA & SAT/ACT score requirements of the NCAA Clearinghouse AND the admission criteria of the college/university, you may want to consider applying to that school. You may be eligible for scholarship money, MAYBE!

Also, some college coaches like to receive emails from the student, and especially the coach of the student. When emailing a coach, you may want to do the following:

- First, greet the coach by his/her name.
- Include your name, grade, stats, GPA, SAT or ACT scores, and also let them know if you have registered for the NCAA Clearinghouse.
- Sending an unedited tape or website video might be a good thing to do, as well.

There are a lot of things to know about the NCAA process. Please do your research and/or ask your child's high school athletic director and coaches for assistance.

Chapter Six

Finding The Right College

With more than 3,600 colleges and universities from which to choose, it's hard to know where exactly to start. Like I've said many times before, I had no idea of how to tackle this college maze.

If I knew then what I know now, I would have insisted we attend more college fairs and tours to see what was "out there". With so many colleges and universities from which to choose, we did not give ourselves a chance to visit more colleges to learn what others had to offer. My son attended his first college of choice, and my daughter attended her third or fourth choice, which happened to be a career-focused school that was perfect for her.

Most students want to go as far away from home as possible, or so they think! What the students do not realize is the further you go away, the more costly it may be. Out-of-state tuition at some colleges is double the cost of in-state tuition. Also, how many times will your child come home per year? Holidays? Spring Break? Will they have to take a plane, train, bus, or drive? How much will that cost per year? What if your child gets sick and has to be hospitalized? How much will it cost for you to get there, hotel fees, food, medical bills, etc.?

My son went to a college two and a half hours away. He didn't have a car in college. When he wanted to come home, we would drive the five-hour roundtrip or he would come with a friend. One thing we hated was transporting our son's belongings home every semester because the dorms were cleaned in between semesters. We would have to load everything up to bring it all back with us, and then a month later, we took everything back down there. That was a pain in the butt!

If I knew then what I know now, I would have invested in a storage place somewhere in the area of the college. Please check with the college to see if students have to take their belongings home each semester. If so, you may want to add storage space to your expense budget.

One thing I found to be very helpful was our involvement in most of this process. Parents, you must be involved in this process! Your involvement in high school is just as important as your involvement in elementary school. You must play a vital role in your child's education and where your child will attend college, because YOU are the person(s) who will most likely pay a majority of the tuition bill. Do not leave this decision up to your child only. Students may choose a college just because of the name or because their friends are going to that particular school. I repeat, YOU, the parent, must be involved in this process!

If there is a college tour that your child wants to attend, make sure you go, as well, or at least have them give you information about all of the colleges they plan to visit. Also, parents, please do not get upset when I say this, but just because a college or university was good for you and other members of your family does not mean it will be a great school for your child. Remember that!

Had I known back then, one of the first things I would have done with my children was to have them think about everything they wanted. For example:

1) Did they want to attend in state or out of state? If out of state, how many miles away?

2) Based on our heart-to-heart conversation, which college's price range best fits the budget? (Keep in mind that you may receive scholarships, grants, and loans to help with the cost of attendance.)

$5,000.00—$10,000.00 per year
$11,000.00—$20,000.00 per year
$21,000.00—$40,000.00 per year
$41,000.00—$60,000.00 per year
Over $61,000.00 per year

Note: I would not have ruled out private colleges because of the cost. Private colleges may cost more than public colleges, but some may give generous scholarships to those who qualify.

3) Would they like to attend a college that has the following student population:

1,000-5,000 (small)
6,000-15,000 (med)
Over 16,000 (large)

4) Does the college have to be in the city, just outside the city, or in a country setting?
5) Does gender matter to them? Same gender or coed?
6) Other things to consider:

    a. Class size
    b. Student to teacher ratio
    c. Accessible to shopping and public transportation
    d. Athletic events on campus
    e. NCAA Divisions I, II or III
    f. Social Life
    g. IEP and 504 Accommodations

h. Study Abroad Programs
i. Dorm rooms, same gender or coed?

These are just a few things that come to mind when trying to find the right college. Students, you will spend a lot of time on campus, so you must decide if it fits your needs.

Does your child have an IEP or 504 Plan? If so, what accommodations or services does the college provide?

The following is a true story of a family who searched for a college to fit their child's special education needs. We have kept the family's name anonymous to protect their privacy.

Mr. & Mrs. X had to find a college that would meet the needs of their son. Mr & Mrs. X says, *"Now more than ever, parents of special needs students understand that their child who has a Learning Disability, Attention Deficit Disorder with or without Hyperactivity, Deafness, Blindness, Asperger's Syndrome or any of the Autism related Spectrum Disorders, can go to college. No longer are vocational schools or group home living situations the only option. Choosing a college for a graduating senior who has special needs is akin to finding the proverbial needle in a haystack. Most schools say that they offer some type of Student Support Services program or services but they are not always what they seem. If we would have known then what we know now, we would have started our college search much sooner, probably around middle school, that would have given us the opportunity to visit more places and programs. Parents and caregivers of a young person with special needs should always be sure to keep all necessary evaluations up to date. Colleges will not consider an application to be complete unless it contains a current Individualized Education Program (IEP). An IEP is a document that is a tailor made educational plan for students that receive special education services as outlined in the Individuals with Disabilities Education Act (IDEA). The IEP contains the student's current level of progress in terms of strengths and developmental opportunities and outlines specific activities, goals, and support services that will assist* students in progressing toward their goals. Parents also need a copy of their student's most recent Psycho-Educational evaluation, one that is less than three years old. Psycho-Educational evaluations contain a battery of tests that offer insight into your students intellectual, cognitive, as well as socio-emotional abilities. The evaluator will often travel to your student's current school and converse with the student's teachers and service providers to get a complete picture of the student's skill-sets. Beware that these evaluations are not cheap. The average Psycho-Educational evaluation costs around two-thousand dollars however most parents will not have to come out of pocket. If the student has been identified for special education services as outlined in their IEP their local school system will be responsible for the costs of that evaluation.

Transcripts and a current copy of the student's high school diploma or G.E.D will also accompany the application. Keep in mind that some colleges will actually waive SAT/ACT scores for students who have special needs. Also please check with your local Department of Disability Services to find out if they offer any assistance in terms of funding and resources, they may help with covering tuition costs or they may offer assistive/adaptive technology to college bound students. Remember to help your young person to advocate for themselves. Explain to them what their disability entails and in turn help them to explain it to others. Most college admissions counselors will possibly allow parents in the room but they may only address the student in the interview. This part may be the hardest part of the whole process as most parents have gotten use to advocating for their student and will now be relegated to the role of the silent partner. Be confident that you have prepared your student to be their own voice in their education. This is all part of the maturation process and it is perfectly natural.

Figure out with your student which settings work best for his/her learning style. Will he/she be better suited for a larger/smaller educational setting? Does my student want to stay closer to home and commute to our local college? Or do they wish to go away and become a residential student? Be mindful that when colleges boasts smaller class sizes that will give your young person more individualized instruction, actually go visit if you can and count chairs and desks in a classroom. How can they accurately make that boast if a classroom has 100 chairs? Check out the dining hall. Students with disabilities may also have food allergies so parents have to be careful of what food options are made available to their student. Examine the dormitories. Look for things that may impact your student such as sleeping quarters, places to study, bathing areas. Some of the larger dorms can contain a lot of high traffic and noise, whereas a smaller dorm setting may help reduce distractibility issues. Look at the layout of the overall school. Most special needs students learn best by routine. Geographically will my student have the ease of moving from classrooms to the library and to the dorm? What is the surrounding environment around the university? It can range from a bustling metropolis to a quiet farm community.

Another insider's tip is to go visit with the Disability Support Services office of the college. Check to see their days/times of service. Do they offer services after hours or on weekends when students may need assistance? Find out if the costs of services are included in the tuition or if that is a separate cost. Ask them how often they meet with students and if the services are only available to new students as some programs only offer support to students within their first two years of college.

Find out if there are schools that specifically cater to the student's specific need. It should be noted that YES, there are colleges designed for the Learning Disabled, members of the Deaf Community, those diagnosed with ADHD and many more. You can never begin your college search too soon. The sooner you start your search the more options you can create for your student. Use all available tools at your disposal. Pick the brain of your student's service provider. Garner advice from your educational advocate. Perform plenty of research on the internet. Attend college fairs armed with questions about how they offer services to students with special needs. For students with special needs there is no one size fits all educational setting that will work for every young person with similar diagnoses *but with proper vetting parents can find the best option available for their special needs student.* Thank you, Mr. and Mrs. X for this very informative information.

Parents, this is worth mentioning again. Please plan to visit the campus with your children. This is very important because once you step on the grounds of the campus, you will know in a matter of hours, if not minutes, if this is the place for your child.

My daughter and I visited a college that was ten hours away. I'm not going to disclose the college for a lot of reasons. We toured the college campus with tour guides, and then we spent time on our own touring the campus without the tour guides. We visited the cafeteria, ate the food, and talked with current students because we wanted to hear the good, the bad, and the ugly. We sat in on a lecture and looked at the computers in the classrooms and the beds and furniture in the dorm. We spoke with the financial aid office to get an idea of how much we would have to pay out of pocket. It was very costly!

We decided we didn't like the campus. The pictures on the website were beautiful, but it was a totally different look when we stepped on campus. The reason why I did not want to disclose the college is because the school was not right for my daughter, but that does not mean it's not right for someone else.

We did the same thing for my son, and it was a great way for both of us to see what the college had to offer in and out of the classrooms. I can vividly remember how well kept the grounds were at the university my son attended. We were told that students were fined if caught walking on the grass. The university has received awards because of the awesome landscaping. The campus was everything my son wanted. It was in a little town far away from city life, and that's what my son wanted. Very little distractions! He fit in well on campus, had great roommates, got involved with the women's bowling league as a volunteer coaching assistant, and worked in the brand-new bowling center on campus. Things went well for him, and it met his needs. However, financially, we struggled.

So, parents, as you can see, there may be some things that fit and some things that don't. But, for us, the good outweighed the bad, and we made our decision to let him attend the college that was right for him.

I want to tell you about an awesome website! It's called ***www. CollegeWeekLive.com***. (If this website is no longer available, search for other websites that provide virtual college tours) This organization provides virtual college tours online. You can sit in the comfort of your home, school, or library and check out thousands of colleges around the world. It's absolutely free! They will feature various colleges throughout the year. College Week Live hosts two large online college fairs in the spring and fall that feature hundreds of colleges, admissions representatives, financial aid officers, current students, and more. They also provide chats where you can type in your answer during the live presentation and the featured representative may answer your question immediately. Isn't that cool! Not only that, but they will also have NCAA representatives, college counselors, etc. online to assist you. One of the best options I love is the archive link. If you missed a college or university presentation, you may be able to go into the archive section to view a recording of it. Check it out today! There should be some archived presentations available of colleges and other educational representatives. This website is awesome. Please register. Again, it's absolutely free!

Chapter Seven

Get To Know Your Child's Counselor Now!

Parents, I cannot stress how important it is for you to be involved with your child's selection of school courses. Do not leave this up to the teachers and counselors only! Get involved! You need to contact your child's school in January or February to find out when they are going to start selecting courses for the next year. Yes, this process starts early at some schools. If your child is a middle school student, you need to work closely with his or her school if they are matriculating (in this case, moving from middle school to high school). You want to be involved in your child's selection of courses to make sure they are correct. You know your child better than anyone. You, the teacher, and the counselor must play a part in choosing the right courses according to the child's strengths and weaknesses. You want to make sure they are being challenged in their strong subjects and also make sure they are getting the assistance in those weaker subjects.

Mrs. Jamila Corria, a school counselor, says this about course selection:

"Many families may not understand the importance of the course selection process. However, this process is the "STARTING POINT" of a student's high school career, and it involves careful planning. WHY? The decisions made establish the precedent for a student's academic development. This is not to imply that the decisions cannot be changed, but to express the importance of making well-informed decisions prior to selecting courses. Remember, thedecisionsmadewill have a huge impact not only on your child's academic development, but also on the availability of future opportunities.

So, what's involved in the process? The answer is simple: I.P.A.D. No, not the electronic tablet, but I.P.A.D.—Individual Planning, Assessment, and Destination. 'I Plan and Assess progress towards reaching the Destination.'

"I"—The Individual

The process must begin with a clear understanding of all of the components that characterize your child. You may be questioning if this is really necessary, but it is! You want to ensure that the best decisions are made to advance your child to the next level of his or her overall development. Let's face it, as quickly as high school begins, it ends and life continues on. While it is important for students to enjoy the experience of high school, it is just as important for students to explore concepts of "self" as it relates to future aspirations. What are your child's interests and talents? Define his or her character, assets, and challenges. What does he or she value the most? What are his or her academic, career, and personal goals? Understanding your child as the Individual should be considered when selecting classes, especially pertaining to the selection of elective classes.

"P"—The Planning

Now that the "Individual" has been identified, let's explore "Planning". As stated earlier, the process of course selection should be "handled with care". Think of the "Planning" as a road map guiding students from Point A (current status in high/middle school) to Point B (desired outcome/future destination). Have you ever taken a long distance road trip to an unfamiliar place without a road map, GPS, or written/printed directions? More than likely, some planning took place to ensure that you knew how to get there, the distance of the trip, costs (especially with today's gas prices), and the amount of time it would take to get there. When selecting courses, think about what you have learned about your child from completing the "Individual" step and how the selected courses will aid your child in achieving educational and personal goals. When "Planning", allow room for "road bumps" along the way. In other words, have an alternate plan. Plan ahead in situations where courses are eliminated due to low enrollment, staffing, or budgetary issues. Plan ahead for the worst-case scenario—your child fails a class!

*So, how do you plan for course selections? Parents and students should be well versed in the graduation requirements. This includes an understanding of the number of credits a student must earn in each required academic category (i.e., math, science, health, elective, etc...), community service obligations, and state standardized testing mandates. For college-bound students, I recommend also examining the admissions requirements of the colleges and universities and programs of interests early on. **DO NOT WAIT** until your child's junior or senior year to do this! Starting this process early on in a student's high school career will allow him or her to select courses that will provide exposure, insight, and experience in areas of interests. Furthermore, it will expand his or her knowledge base, develop skills, and perhaps serve as motivation to perform well throughout his or her high school career. This idea can also be applied to career-bound students.*

Employers are seeking individuals with a specific set of skills to perform tasks for a given position. The courses taken in high school can help to develop the set of skills needed to perform within the position. To further explain, let's use the example of a student interested in a career as a cosmetologist or medical technician. Both careers require an in-depth understanding and application of Science. Courses that will provide a great foundation for careers in the two areas are Chemistry and Biology. Although the planning process may seem extensive, exasperating, and even complicated, the consequence of NOT developing a plan could result in missed opportunities and affect a student's personal, academic, and career development. *"Plan early for success later!"*

"A"—The Assessment

The final course selections should be reflective of a student's aptitude, knowledge, and interests. Additionally, the selected courses should provide opportunities for a student to further develop his or her critical and analytical skills. School personnel determine course selections based on a number of factors to include: teacher recommendation and feedback, earned grade, score on various assessments, and parent/student requests. Prior to making any course requests, parents should also conduct an assessment of their child's performance. Examine earned grades and feedback provided by teachers on report cards. Review scores and recommendations provided on assessments. Ask your child for his or her opinion of their performance in each class and solicit feedback about course recommendations. Schedule an appointment with school personnel (in many cases, the appointment should be scheduled with the school counselor) to ask questions, discuss concerns, or request assistance with selecting the appropriate courses. Take into consideration the needs of your child by asking, "What support will my child need to be successful in this course? What supports are currently in place within the school and home community?" This may mean acquiring tutoring support, arranging study sessions with peers/teachers after school, allocating additional time for studying and assignment completion, assisting with organization, applying new methods of studying, and increasing communication with school personnel (just to name a few).

"Want Honors or AP?"

In today's competitive academic market, students are faced with the pressure of enrolling in Honors level and Advanced Placement (AP) level courses throughout their high school careers. However, precaution should be taken to ensure that the student has the aptitude, skills, and support to meet the challenges of Honors and AP level courses. In other words, the goal should not be the ability to enroll in such courses alone, but in the student's ability to be successful in such courses. In cases where a student is not academically prepared for the rigor of an Honors or AP level course (yet has a desire to experience the challenge of such courses), it is beneficial to collaborate with school personnel to determine the best method to develop the student for the demand of Honors and AP level courses. Through this comprehensive assessment, parents can gain a better understanding of their child's current status. In turn, the Planning process is made easier.

"D"—The Destination

The Destination or ultimate goal for any high school student is to earn the high school diploma. No student wishes to spend an additional summer, semester, or year in high school. In fact, there are instances where students earn their high school diploma prior to their anticipated graduation date! Walk through any hallway in any high school in the nation and you will hear shouts of "I can't wait to graduate!" However, the goal for parents is to ensure that their children are equipped with the skills and ability to succeed in high school and beyond. Therefore, selecting the right courses is essential in equipping students with the competency to achieve short-term and long-term life goals. Remember, when a student earns a high school diploma, it means that he or she has acquired the necessary foundational skills to perform basic functions and tasks as a productive member of society. The "foundational skills" can only be acquired if the appropriate courses (including On-level/Regular, Honors, and AP levels) are selected.

Keep in mind that earning a high school diploma is one of many goals that a student will have throughout their lifetime. The Destination is ever-changing and on-going. It IS the process of completion and initiation. In other words, when one goal or "Destination" has been reached, a new journey begins. Thus, the I.P.A.D. process repeats itself as the Individual evolves from one Destination to another.

All in all, the process of course selection is an important part of the student's high school career. It sets the foundation for a student's development throughout his or her high school career. As discussed, it involves components that must be cautiously and thoroughly examined and reviewed throughout a student's high school career. More importantly, the decisions should not be the sole responsibility of school personnel. Instead, the decision–making process should be a joint endeavor with school personnel. In all course selection decisions, ask the following: "Will this lead my child closer to his or her destination?" and "What support will my child need along this journey?"

If I knew then what I know now, I would have spoken with my children's teachers about their strengths and weaknesses. I did ask questions like, "How are my children doing?" When the teacher responded that they were doing very well, I would respond, "Oh great," and that was it. There should have been more conversation on my part. Things like, "Tell me how I can best help my child stay on task? What type of college major do you think would 'best fit' my child based on your academic knowledge of them? Should I stress more reading and writing? Can you recommend any books that my children might find interesting? Should we consider any Honors or AP classes for my children?"

If I knew then what I know now, I would have asked the counselor, When should they really start practicing the PSAT or SAT/ACT or both? Do you have a list of scholarships or a website available so that we (my children and I) can start researching them? Should we give you a resume or a list of activities that my children participate in both inside and outside of school? How important is community service? What types of community service are colleges looking? Are my children in the right courses based on their strengths and what they may want to major? When should I attend financial aid meetings? Should I start saving for my children's college education now? Are scholarships really available? What colleges best fit my child? What about my pocket?"

If I knew then what I know now, I would have helped my children create a resume and/or "brag sheet" and handed it to their counselor at the end of their junior year or beginning of their senior year. The resume or brag sheet describes everything students are involved in during their high school years, both in and out of school. The brag sheet describes each activity in detail. The resume should be a brief description of the brag sheet.

The brag sheet helps the counselor, teacher, and others write a great recommendation for your child. This is the time to brag about all of your child's activities and accomplishments. The counselor may know about activities that your child participates in school, but may have no idea that your child is the president of a social group that raises money for low-income students to have backpacks at the beginning of each year. Or that your child has bowled in a youth league since elementary school and is an awesome bowler who averages over a 200 bowling score!

As the president of a social group, your child shows leadership skills, responsibility, dependability, etc., and this looks very good on a college recommendation letter. As a bowler in a youth league, for example, your child shows leadership as well as being a team player. The other less detailed resume can be mailed to colleges along with your child's application, transcript, SAT/ACT scores, etc. when applying to the college. It can also be included in scholarship applications.

Chapter Eight

Scholarships

I hear parents and students ask, "Where are all of the scholarships?" If I knew then what I know now, we would have started looking for scholarships early. We would have looked on websites like www.fastweb.com and other scholarship websites if they existed ten years ago.

When it comes to searching for scholarships, you have to plan ahead of time. Boy, I wish I knew this back then! This could have saved us thousands of dollars! If I knew then what I know now, I would not have waited until my children got accepted to college before I started looking. Had I known then, I would have researched every website, book, magazine, etc. Yes, there are scholarships available, but the process to obtain them may take some time, patience, and a lot of work.

Here are some things I would have done differently when researching and applying for scholarships:

1) Searched the internet for scholarships in my children's 9th-12th grade years. There are some scholarships and essay contests available for students who are not high school seniors.
2) Identified the ones that met my children's qualifications.

3) Looked at each essay topic and started my children writing essays ahead of time (even 6-12 months ahead of time).

4) Looked at the organization's website, if available, to see how many students received the scholarships in previous years. This allows you to see how many scholarships may be available each year.

5) Assisted my child by making sure they had completed their part of the application before the deadline date.

6) Filled out general information for them.

7) Emailed teachers and counselors the scholarship recommendation forms early to make sure they had time to complete them. If I could not email them directly, I would fax or send them with my child or go to the school myself. I would follow up with them to see if the paperwork had been completed and then have my child or myself pick them up when ready. (Yes, I would do this for my children, because remember, it's teamwork!)

8) Requested the transcript from the registrar or secretary in advance.

9) Had a box of large envelopes (9 ½ x 12 or 10 ½ x 13) available for mailing, as well as stamps available for postage. Some schools may not have the funds to purchase these items for your children. It's best to be prepared just in case.

10) As a team, we would have placed all applications, recommendations, essays, and transcripts in the envelopes and mailed them or had the school mail them for us. Some schools want to send out all of their scholarship applications, and some teachers and counselors do not allow students to hand carry or mail their recommendations. So, please check with your school ahead of time to know their particular process.

This is also helpful for the college application process. Instead of mailing the scholarship application, mail the college application using the same procedure. It is important to note here that there may be scholarship and college application deadline dates at your child's high school. For example, a college or scholarship application deadline could be December 1st, but the high school's application deadline is November 10th, which is three weeks (excluding holidays) **before** the college's deadline. This means the school personnel (registrar, secretary, teacher, counselors, etc.) need time to complete recommendation forms, transcript requests, etc. and mail everything to the college on or before their deadline date. Using this same example, if a student waits until November 25th to give the school personnel a scholarship or college application that needs teacher and counselor recommendations and transcripts mailed with it, it is possible the recommendations and transcript may not get mailed on time to meet the December 1st deadline. Please be aware of that. You do not want your application to be incomplete. Some colleges are lenient and understand that teachers and counselors are writing a lot of recommendations, but some may not be as understanding. So, don't risk it! Remember, teachers and counselors may write recommendations for a lot more students than your child. I could add more, but I will stop here because I am trying to keep this book short, simple, and to the point.

There are academic and merit-based scholarships that come directly from the college. This is where the REAL money is, ladies and gentlemen! There are qualifications and criteria that must be met, but, students, if you plan early, study hard, and practice the PSAT, SAT or ACT, you may be a candidate for some HUGE money! Students can receive up to full tuition, room, board, books, fees, and some even offer laptops and other educational tools. I personally know students who have received over $200,000 (over four years) in academic or merit-based scholarships!

If I knew then what I know now, I would have definitely searched this website earlier. We waited entirely too late! Parents, parents, parents, I cannot stress this enough. Please start your research early and learn what's available to your children early. When I say early, I'm talking about elementary school. I am so serious and passionate about this. I don't want anyone to make the same mistakes I did.

Please hear me! I want every child to succeed and every parent to be able to send their child to the post-secondary educational institution that's best for them. That's the main reason why I wrote this book! I want to provide parents and students nationwide with as much information as possible. Why? This is my gift, my passion. I hope this book will help get the word out to the world.

Chapter Nine

FAFSA—Free Application For Federal Student Aid

If I knew then what I know now, I would have asked for assistance when I completed this form. This was the form from you-know-where! As I said before, the FAFSA form was not available online, and it had over one hundred questions on it. I have no idea if I filled this form out correctly. What if I filled it out incorrectly? What if my EFC wasn't $10,004! What if it were much less? Well, there is nothing I can do that will change my circumstances now, but there sure is something you can do. Learn from my mistakes!

The FAFSA form is now available online at *www.fafsa. gov*. There are not as many questions as before, and it's more user-friendly. If I had to do it again, I would definitely seek help. All parents of students who want to attend college should fill out this form. According to the *www.studentaid.ed.gov* website, there's over 150 billion dollars available in scholarships, grants, work study, and loans from the federal government for over 14 million people who plan to attend college. In order to receive the funds, you must fill out the FAFSA form. The form must be filled out every year that your child attends college.

You can receive an estimate of how much you may be able to receive in financial aid by going to **www.fafsa4caster.ed.gov.** Just put in the information requested and you will receive an estimate. Unlike the FAFSA online form that can only be filled out during the student's senior year of high school, you can receive an estimate at any time. This will help you plan accordingly. If you need assistance with this, please call the Federal Student Aid Help Desk at **1-800-4-FED-AID (1-800-433-3243) or 319-337-5665.**

Never assume that you will not qualify for financial aid. Private and public colleges are different, and each school that you apply to may have a different income level that's used to provide scholarships to students. Just because your results from the FAFSA comes back and states you are not "Pell Grant" (or any other type of grant) eligible, it doesn't mean you do not qualify for other grants, work study, loans, or college scholarships and/or grants that may be available.

I am not happy about having loans, but I can say I would rather have my loans from the federal government than any other banking institution. Their interest rates are lower than most other financial institutions, and they will work with you if you can't pay due to unforeseen circumstances. I look at student loans this way: The federal government provided the funds for us because we did not have the money available to send our children to college or career school. They provided the funds for us so that my son could go to college. However, after he graduated or stopped going at least part time, they wanted their money back so others can have the opportunity to go to college. I must say, I was hesitant about giving the school all of my personal information and applying for loans, but we did what we had to do.

Parents and students may find the form a bit complicated to fill out, but there are organizations available to assist you with completing it. There is the FAFSA assistance hotline available to you on the fafsa.gov website. Also, some states host an event in January and February called College Goal Sunday. This event is held on a Sunday for two or three hours at a college or other facility to help parents and students fill out the FAFSA form. It is absolutely free. Check out their website at *www.collegegoalsundayusa.org.* If you have general questions about financial aid, contact someone at the federal student aid office at *www.studentaid.ed.gov.* The toll free number is 1-800-433-3243.Parents, I hope you consider filling out the FAFSA form in order for your child to have the best chance of obtaining some type of federal financial aid funding. Again, your child may be awarded scholarships, grants, and/or loans. I know every situation is different, and I am certainly not going to start judging you for your decisions, but I will say that your child really needs you right now. I know loans can accrue a lot of debt. Maybe you can make an agreement with your child or have them sign a notarized contract saying they will help you pay off their college debt if you have to take out a loan. Parents, please help your children the best way you can. If you could not save for college, the federal government may assist you with a loan for your child to go to college, but you must pay it back.

There may be other financial forms to fill out. The CSS Profile is a financial form that some colleges prefer instead and sometimes in addition to the FAFSA. Check with the colleges you are applying for more information

Chapter Ten

How to Find the Best College for Your Buck

If I knew then what I know now, I would have looked into other ways to save money for my children's college education or looked for colleges that may have saved us more money. I know now that there are ways to spend less for college. One way is to have your child attend a two-year college in your area for the first two years. I know some students may be against that because they want to go directly to a four-year college and move away from home, but there are great things happening at community colleges.

Community colleges offer a variety of majors and also provide students an opportunity to attend college at a lower cost than a four-year college. I tell students that if you attend a community college for two years and transfer to a four-year college, when you graduate in two years from the four-year college, your degree looks no different than the student who attended that college for four years. The only difference is that you have probably saved more money, while they may have accrued more debt! So, if funding is an issue, you may want to check with your community college. Talk with the academic advisors and transfer office at the community college to know which course credits are transferrable to four-year colleges. Also ask them for a list of four-year colleges that have accepted all or most of their college credits. This will help you to plan in advance.

Another great way to save money is to attend a public college or university in your state. Most of the time, a public college or university is less expensive than a private or out-of-state school.

The Academic Common Market!

If you live in any of the states mentioned below, you are in the Academic Common Market area and may be able to attend one of these out-of-state colleges while paying "in state" tuition prices!

On their website (*www.sreb.org*) it says, "For over 35 years, the SREB (Southern Regional Educational Board) Academic Common Market has helped students pursue out-of-state college degrees at discounted tuition rates, through agreements among the states and colleges and universities. Over 1,900 undergraduate and graduate degree programs are available in 16 SREB states." If you live in one of the states mentioned below, please check this out.

Alabama, Arkansas, Delaware, Florida, Georgia, Kentucky, Louisiana, Maryland, Mississippi, North Carolina, Oklahoma, South Carolina, Tennessee, Texas, Virginia, West Virginia. You can find out more about them by going to *www.sreb.org.*

Look for the Academic Common Market link that's usually on the front page of the website. If it's no longer on the front page of the website, search for "Academic Common Market". Under "Search for Programs" click on "Selecting Your Home State and Reviewing the Available Programs." Choose your state, click on "Search for Programs", and then click the "Search" button to see a listing of colleges and specific majors that qualify for the in-state tuition agreement. If you need further assistance, contact the Southern Regional Educational Board at 404-875-9211. If you see colleges and majors of interests, click on the "More Information" field under the major field. You will see the program details and contact persons for the college and your state. You can email your state coordinator from this page if you are interested in more information or an application to apply.

If your children are interested in pursuing certain majors, I hope you will consider looking at this website to see the thousands of majors available. There are requirements to some of the majors. Some states only offer in-state tuition to students who are college juniors, while some states are only offering in-state tuition to graduate students (students pursuing degrees higher than a bachelors degree), but it is worth taking the time to look at what's offered.

Let me give you an example. Shepherd University in West Virginia offered the following majors for 2011-2012 academic year for some out-of-state students in the SREB Academic Common Market: (note: this may change year to year)

- B.F.A. degree in Art with a concentration in Photography and Computer Imagery
- B.S. degree in Computer and Information Sciences with a concentration in Networking and Security
- B.S. degree in Computer and Information Technology with a concentration in Bioinformatics and Information Security
- B.S. degree in Environmental Studies with a concentration in Aquatic Science
- B.S. degree in Environmental Studies with a concentration in Environmental Engineering
- B.S. degree in Environmental Studies with a concentration in Environmental Sustainability
- B.S. degree in Environmental Studies with a concentration in Historic Preservation
- B.A. degree in History with a concentration in Civil War and 19th Century America
- B.S. degree in Recreation and Leisure Studies with a concentration in Sports Communication
- B.S. degree in Recreation and Leisure Studies with a concentration in Sports Marketing

- B.S. degree in Recreation and Leisure Studies with a concentration in Athletic Coaching and Officiating
- B.A degree in History with a concentration in Public History
  Here's what the acronyms mean:
- B.F.A. (Bachelors of Fine Arts)
- B.S. (Bachelors of Science)
- B.A. (Bachelors of Arts)

The total cost of attendance:

In-State Tuition & Fees	$5,554
Room and Board	$8,466
Total Costs	$14,020

Wow! If I knew then what I know now, I would have had my son and daughter look into this school I had no idea it existed. I must admit, maybe I was given the information and just didn't follow through. I remember collecting so many brochures, pamphlets, and books during the financial aid workshops I attended, but it was too overwhelming to read it all. My son is an IT Specialist and would have been able to pursue one of the degrees in computer and information sciences or technology if they were available then. See, there are ways to pay for college. We just have to tap into the right places.

Parents, if you live in any of the sixteen states mentioned, I pray you look into the Academic Common Market. Again, some states may not offer the program to undergraduates, but it is definitely worth looking into. Make sure to check the website yearly as majors and funding may change from year to year for this program.

Also, for students living in the following states, the Western Interstate Commission for Higher Education (WICHE) program may be available to you: Alaska, Arizona, California, Colorado, Hawaii, Idaho, Montana, New Mexico, Nevada, North Dakota, Oregon, South Dakota, Utah, Washington, and Wyoming. Go to *www.wiche.edu* for more information.

If you do not live in these states, there may be neighboring state colleges near you that offer discounted tuition. It's worth a try to ask your neighboring state colleges or universities.

Chapter Eleven

Counting up the Cost

My son and daughter are in their thirties, and we still have loans left to pay! They have loans to pay, as well! If I knew then what I know now, I would have started saving for college much earlier.

I would have started saving as soon as the doctor said, "Congratulations, you're expecting!" Start planning for your child's future early. Start putting $5, $10, $20 or more aside weekly or monthly in a college fund at a bank or a tax-sheltered annuity. Most states offer college savings plans. Do not put any accounts in your children's name. They should be the beneficiaries. This will make more sense when you start to complete the FAFSA (Free Application For Federal Student Aid) form in their senior year of high school.

One of the biggest mistakes I made was spending money that I could have saved. There were times when I would eat fast food everyday for breakfast, lunch, and sometimes dinner. That adds up to a lot of money. My husband would say to me, "Cynthia, I want you to write down everything you spend in a day and calculate it for one week." I wouldn't do it. I didn't want to see how much I was spending. I felt that I worked hard and should be able to spend what I wanted to spend. Well, that kind of thinking was totally wrong and ended up costing me later in life. So, if I knew then what I know now,

I would have definitely listened to my husband and started saving more; not just for college, but also for other things we wanted.

The following is an example of how much money I could have saved if I started when my children were infants, as well as an example of how much we spent in a week just on fast food, snacks, etc. I estimated how much it would be over eighteen years, because our children were eighteen or close to it when they graduated. Use whatever calculation works for you.

If we had saved $5 per week for 52 weeks per year x 18 years, we would have had $4,680 saved for college, ($5 x 52 weeks = $260.00 x 18 years = $4,680)

If we had saved $10 per week for 52 weeks per year x 18 years, we would have saved $9,360. ($10 x 52 weeks = $520.00 x 18 years = $9,360)

If we had saved $20 per week for 52 weeks per year x 18 years, we would have saved $18,720.00. ($20 x 52 weeks = $1040.00 x 18 years = $18,720.00) Not bad!

If I knew then what I know now, I wouldn't have spent so much on fast food. Imagine this, I estimate I spent $3 on breakfast and $5 on lunch five days a week and may have eaten out for dinner three times a week, spending $10 on my meal each time. (This is an estimate. Remember, this was ten years or so ago, and prices are much higher today). Now, let's add that up:

- $3 for breakfast 5 days a week for 52 weeks x 18 years = $14,040
- $5 for lunch 5 days a week for 52 weeks x 18 years = $23,400
- $10 for dinner 3 days a week for 52 weeks x 18 years = $28,080

It adds up to $65,520.00 that I spent on fast food, snacks, etc. for eighteen years! That's an estimate. It could be less or more depending on how much I spent per day. I remember spending $8 for lunch on a salad. Imagine how much money I could have saved for my children's college fund if I would have bought a box of cereal, bread, and lunchmeat to eat at work and cooked a casserole at home instead of eating out!

And, check this out! If my husband spent the same on his breakfast, lunch, and dinner for eighteen years, we would have spent over $131,000.00! Amazing! Well, I might as well make you sick. What if you added your children's fast food expenses to that? How many of you are doing that now? If you are, please consider stopping or at least cutting it down.

Please consider the advice of my husband. Write down everything you spend for one week. Multiply it by 52 weeks in a year, and then multiply it by the number of years your child or children have left in school before going to college. If your child is in 8th grade, you would multiply by four because he/she has four years left before college. See how much you may be able to save? Do not make the mistakes I did! Please!

I'll give you another good example. Cell phones, how much are they costing you per month? Per year? Multiply that by the number of years your child has before attending college, and look at how much you could save. I'm not saying don't have cell phones, but maybe look for a cheaper plan. There are so many things I spent money on that I didn't really need. Where can you cut back on spending?

I am guessing the average cost of attendance (tuition, room and board, fees, books, transportation) at a public college/university is approximately $15,000-$20,000 per year. Private colleges and universities in the United States may cost approximately $30,000.00-$70,000.00 per year. Some are over $70,000.00 per year! Please learn from our mistakes and try to save as much as you can. I know times may be hard for a lot of us, but do the best you can to put a little aside.

If I knew then what I know now, I would have started a college fund for all of the children in my sibling's family. I know of a large family that started a family scholarship fund. All of the family members who contribute are able to use portions of the money to send their children to college. What a great idea! Grandparents and parents of children can start their own College 529 savings program. There is a website, *www.savingforcollege.com,* that gives information about this program, as well as other college saving plans. Choose the savings plan that best suits your budget.

Chapter Twelve

Professional Judgment & Appeal Letters

If I knew then what I know now, I would have spoken with someone in the financial aid office and told them that we had some other expenses that may help us lower or adjust our EFC. Even though EFCs may not be changed technically, the college could've recalculated figures that could have helped reduce our out-of-pocket expenses. One huge expense was the private high school tuition we had to pay for our children. I had no idea college financial aid advisors could make a professional judgment about extenuating circumstances. Extenuating circumstances are referred to as high medical costs not covered by insurance, job loss, death of a spouse, and private school expenses, just to name a few. The college financial aid advisors may take into consideration some of these expenses and recalculate your income figures, which could lead to a lower amount of out-of-pocket expenses for you.

It is a good idea to talk with someone in the college financial aid office and then follow up with a personal letter via email, mail, or fax to the person you spoke with on the phone. Why didn't I know this? I had an extenuating circumstance! Why didn't someone say something? (And yes, I'm venting!)

Back to professional judgment, due to the current economic crisis, college financial aid advisors may take into consideration your extenuating circumstances. College financial aid officers are allowed to make professional judgments on an individual basis. I assisted a parent in Atlanta who needed a letter like this. She was self-employed, and due to the economy, her salary took a tremendous cut. After we submitted a letter with documentation of the change in income to the financial aid officer at her child's college, the mother was able to receive a reduction of a few thousand dollars off of her child's tuition, which made it affordable for her to pay the balance.

Oh, one important thing: Keep a copy of everything! Colleges handle a lot of college applications, medical records, and financial documentation, and sometimes papers may get misplaced. Please, please, keep a copy of everything you send the college just in case you need documentation later. The great thing about modern technology is that you can send mostly everything electronically, which gives you a copy of your information for your files.

Parents, if you do not understand any of this financial stuff, please ask for assistance. The school counselors may know. If not, please seek advice from one of the college financial aid officers of the college your child plans to attend. You can also seek help at *www.studentaid.ed.gov.* Send them an email or call them at 1-800-4FE-DAID (1-800-433-3243) or TTY 1-800-730-8913.

Chapter Thirteen

Moms and Dads Always Keep Tissue Handy!

A couple of days before my son left for college, we were in a department store getting all of his things for school. I was so excited for him and us. I can remember the day like it was yesterday. I got everything I thought he needed: sheets, pillowcases, a trunk, school supplies, etc. I was standing in line waiting to pay for the things I had in my shopping cart, when I turned around and saw the cutest little brown teddy bear. As I held the fluffy, soft, cute stuffed animal in my hands, memories of holding my son for the first time in the hospital after delivery made me smile, and all of a sudden, I began to weep uncontrollably.

"My son is leaving me!" I cried. "Oh my God! What am I going to do?"

My daughter had a job and her own apartment. So, there would be no one left at the house but my husband and me. Heck, I didn't even know who he was anymore. Our children were our life! All of these thoughts rushed through my mind all of a sudden, and as I stood there crying, people were staring at me like I was crazy. My husband walked up and stared at me in shock, thinking I was in pain or something, until I said, "My baby is going to college and leaving me!"

Tears were streaming down my face and I didn't have any tissue! Finally, a very nice lady gave me some tissue. I wiped my face, blew my nose, and pulled myself together long enough to pay for the stuff and get the heck out of the store. It hit me all of a sudden. I thought I was fine with it, but I wasn't. How could I let my son leave me? We were a very close family. When my daughter moved to her own apartment, I cried, too! It was like I was losing my best friend, and I was!

I was warned a year before that this would happen. Two of our friend's children went to college a year before ours. I will never forget the time I called one of my friends just to say hello, and she burst into tears while saying "I am going to miss him so much." When I asked who was it that she would miss, she replied, "My son. He's leaving today, and I don't know what I'm going to do without him." I talked with her for a while, assuring her everything would be okay. An hour later, I was talking with another mother whose child was about to leave for college, and the same thing happened. She started crying and saying the same thing. When I hung up the phone, I said to my husband, "Okay, that's it. Our son is not going away to college because I am not going through the same thing those two are going through." But guess what? I did! So, if I knew then what I know now, I would have kept a box of tissue in my purse just in case of embarrassing, but awesome moments like that!

I will never forget telling my husband that I didn't think I could stay in the house anymore because it was going to be too quiet. However, it has become the best place on earth! My husband and I started dating again. We finally got a chance to take a vacation. Actually several vacations! Parents, you will have a tough time at first, but believe me, you will get used to your children not being at home. I can remember the first holiday break my son came home from college. He stayed up all night and slept all day. His friends were in and out of the house, and my husband and I were exhausted going to work every morning because of the constant talking and laughing of my son and his friends. Even though we truly enjoyed all of them, we began to cherish the times when he was away at college!

Resources

My website, blog and more!
http://www.collegeandcareeradvice.com/
(student business cards, mailing labels)

ROTC Programs
http://www.goarmy.com/rotc.html http://www.navy.com/
joining/education-opportunities/nrotc.html http://officer.
marines.com/marine/making_marine_officers/cp1/
nrotc?WT.mc_id=TODAYSMILITARYOFFROTC
http://www.afrotc.com/

www.fastweb.com & www.scholarshipsonline.org
(scholarships)

www.naviance.com (Family Connections)Costs a fee to join
Scholarships, career interest surveys, college search, etc.

www.collegeboard.org
Scholarships, SAT/PSAT prep, SAT I & SAT II registration, college
search, CSS Profile financial aid application

www.act.org
ACT registration & PLAN prep

www.nextstepu.com
(Scholarships) College information

www.collegedata.com
College information: Cost, Majors, Financial Aid/ Scholarships, etc.

www.ncaa.org
NCAA Information & registration for student athletes

www.collegeweeklive.com
Online virtual college tours

www.sreb.org
Academic Common Market Information

www.studentaid.ed.gov
Great website to help assist parents and students with financial aid questions, FAFSA, etc.

www.revolutionprep.com
SAT/ACT test prep organization.

www.collegegoalsundayusa.org
Assistance with completing the FAFSA

(Some websites may no longer be available)

Fundraising opportunities may be available to schools, parent organizations and nonprofits that provide educational resources to students. Please contact *hammonddavisllc@yahoo.com* for more information on how this book may provide funding for your organization.

Praise for
If I Knew Then, What I Know Now!

This book was so informative and such a quick, easy read! It really opened my eyes to the many things that I need to start doing now, and things I wish I had started doing sooner. I have one son who is getting ready to start his senior year of high school in the fall, and I will start looking into scholarships and financial aid this week. I also have two other sons, and I plan on following the advice laid out in this book! Cynthia is obviously passionate about helping parents and students succeed with the college process, and her passion, sensitivity, and humor really shine through in this book. Clearly, this is the path that has been laid out for her by God.

Vicky E.
Parent & School Teacher/Educator

Cynthia really knows what she is talking about in this book. It has opened my eyes tremendously. In these short chapters, I've learned so much on how to prepare myself to take the right path toward my children's future college education. At one point, I thought I was prepared to send my oldest son to college. God, I was wrong! Cindy, I want to thank you for showing and giving me the opportunity to prepare myself better before sending my youngest son to college.

Thank you for all the wise tips you merge in your book. I enjoyed your book and am looking for another wise book such as this book to come forward . . . Celly

Cynthia en realidad sabe lo que está hablando su libro. Si yo hubiera sabido lo que ahora se me abierto los ojos tremendamente. En estos cortos capítulos, he aprendido demasiado cómo prepararme para tomar camino correcto hacia una mejor carrera universitaria para mis hijos. En un momento pensé que ya estaba lista para enviar a mi hjio mayor a la universidad, Dios que mal informada estaba yo. Cindy, te quiero agradecer por enseñarme y darme la oportunidad de prepararme mejor antes de enviar a mi hijo menor a la universidad. Gracias por tus sabios consejos que narraste en tu libro. Me divertí muchísimo cuando leí tu libro, espero otro libro sabio como este lo más pronto posible . . .

Aracelly G.
"La educacion es la mejor herencia que un padre puede dejar a sus hijo" Autor desconocido

Mrs. Hammond Davis is truly my biggest role model and motivator. Thank you for all of your guidance and support. I stand where I am today, a $140,000 scholarship recipient, thanks to you! Congratulations on all of your accomplishments. You deserve this and more!

Stephanie V.
College Student

"Our daughter was about to start her senior year of high school, getting ready for college. It was a struggle and starting to take a toll on us. That's when we met Mrs. Hammond-Davis. She's an excellent

guide for both students and their parents on how to apply for college and scholarships that are most suitable for them. She directed our daughter to a foundation that awarded her a $140,000.00 scholarship. Ms Davis is a great resource; she has been a tremendous blessing to our family!"

Bruce and Valencia B.

The college application and financial aid process is a labyrinth of confusion and frustration that can cause much stress in families. I always have said that senior year was worse than childbirth. This is a welcome resource for all parents of students K-12!

Teresa DeGraffenreidt Joiner
Assistant Principal of Academics
Don Bosco *Cristo Rey High School*

Printed in the USA
CPSIA information can be obtained
at www.ICGtesting.com
LVHW050524251123
764788LV00002B/48

9 781936 513338